AF575766

Top Cat Breeds

Persian

Bernard Conaghan

TABLE OF CONTENTS

A Crabtree Seedlings Book

Crabtree Publishing
crabtreebooks.com

School-to-Home Support for Caregivers and Teachers

This book helps children grow by letting them practice reading. Here are a few guiding questions to help the reader with building his or her comprehension skills. Possible answers appear here in red.

Before Reading:

- What do I think this book is about?
  - *I think this book is about what Persian cats look like.*
  - *I think this book is about how Persians act.*
- What do I want to learn about this topic?
  - *I want to learn how Persians act.*
  - *I want to know what Persians look like.*

During Reading:

- I wonder why...
  - *I wonder why they have a lot of fur.*
  - *I wonder why their coats are long and silky.*
- What have I learned so far?
  - *I have learned some Persians are one color.*
  - *I have learned some Persians have a tortoiseshell pattern.*

After Reading:

- What details did I learn about this topic?
  - *I learned their coats need daily brushing.*
  - *I learned Persians are friendly and loving.*
- Read the book again and look for the glossary words.
  - *I see the word **shed** on page 10 and the word **silky** on page 6. The other glossary words are found on pages 22 and 23.*

The Persian is a top cat **breed**!

Its body is heavy.

Persians have a lot of fur too.

Their **coats** are long and **silky**. They feel fluffy.

Photo Fun Fact

Persians have short ears.

Some Persians are one color.

Others have patterns such as **tortoiseshell** or tabby stripes.

Their coats need daily brushing. They **shed** a lot.

Photo Fun Fact

Their fur can get tangled easily.

Exercise is important. These cats love to play with their toys.

Persians need to be fed carefully. They can become **overweight** easily.

Fun Fact

Most Persian cats were **bred** to have flat faces.

Persians are friendly and loving.

Their voices are
soft and quiet.

Persians make great pets. Would you like to **adopt** this top cat breed?

Cat Adoption Quiz

Are you ready to add a cat or kitten to your home? Answer "yes" or "no" to each question.

1. I have a lot of space for a cat.
2. I will feed my cat the right foods every day.
3. I will clean the litter box every day.
4. I will play with my cat daily.
5. I am ok if my things get ruined.
6. I will provide my cat with interesting toys.
7. I will not force my cat to do things.
8. I understand that not all cats like to snuggle.
9. I understand that all kittens grow up to be cats.
10. I will make sure my cat feels safe.

How many "yes" answers do you have?

0–5: You are definitely not ready to adopt. Maybe in a year or two.

6–8: You can start talking about adoption.

9–10: You understand how to be a responsible cat caregiver. You are ready to add a cat to your family.

Cat Playtime

Do

- Make play a daily habit.
- Use wand toys to keep your cat far away so you don't get scratched.
- Make toys from cardboard boxes with entry and exit holes.
- Play with each cat separately if you have more than one cat.
- Pull the "prey" away from the cat and not towards it.

Don't

- Keep a toy in your hand and then tease your cat to get it.
- Encourage play with body parts, such as fingers.
- Place toys close to your cat's face.
- Frustrate your cat by only using laser pointers they can't catch.
- Punish a kitten or cat that scratches or bites during play.

Glossary

adopt (uh-DOPT): To take a pet home and be its caregiver

bred (bred): Created by mating two animals with a particular characteristic

breed (breed): A particular type of animal within a group of animals

coat (koht): The natural fur or hair that covers an animal

overweight (oh-ver-WEYT): Weighing more than normal

shed (shed): To cast off hair

silky (sil-kee) Smooth and soft

tortoiseshell (TAWR-tuhs-shel): A pattern of two colors, such as yellow and black

Index

About the Author

Bernard Conaghan lives in South Carolina with a German shepherd named Duke and a black-and-white rescue cat named Duchess. He is a coach on his son's football team. He always eats one scoop of peach ice cream after dinner.

Written by: Bernard Conaghan
Designed by: Jen Bowers
Series Development: James Earley
Proofreader: Kathy Middleton
Educational Consultant: Marie Lemke M.Ed.

Photographs: Shutterstock: Cover and throughout: ©2012 Ewa Studio, © Nadya_Art, © Studio Ayutaka, © Net Vector, © ANNA_KOVA; p.3 frame © Denis Cristo; p.4 ©2012 Ewa Studio; p.5, 22 ©2011 Eric Isselee; p.6, 23 ©2016 rukawajung; p.7 ©2020 alvarog1970; p.8 ©2011 Eric Isselee; p.9 ©2015 Jagodka, p.9, 23 ©2010 WilleeCole Photography; p.10, 23 ©2022 Savvapanf Photo; p.11 ©2016 ANURAK PONGPATIMET; p.13 ©2017 ANURAK PONGPATIMET; p.15, 22 ©2016 Rutina; p.16 ©2021 Creative Cat Studio; p.17 ©2020 Annette Shaff; p.18, 22 ©2011 Eric Isselee

---

Crabtree Publishing

crabtreebooks.com 800-387-7650

Copyright © 2025 Crabtree Publishing

All rights reserved. No part of this publication may be reproduced, stored in a retrieval system or be transmitted in any form or by any means, electronic, mechanical, photocopying, recording, or otherwise, without the prior written permission of Crabtree Publishing.

Printed in Canada/012024/CP20231127

Published in Canada
Crabtree Publishing
616 Welland Ave.
St. Catharines, Ontario
L2M 5V6

Published in the United States
Crabtree Publishing
347 Fifth Ave
Suite 1402-145
New York, New York 10016

Library and Archives Canada Cataloguing in Publication
Available at the Library and Archives Canada

Library of Congress Cataloging-in-Publication Data
Available at the Library of Congress

Hardcover: 978-1-0398-3843-7
Paperback: 978-1-0398-3928-1
Ebook (pdf): 978-1-0398-4010-2
Epub: 978-1-0398-4082-9